Table of Contents

A Manual On How To Read People Like A Book.

Dr.James bond

Isbn : 978-1-312-39304-2

The Art of Reading People

Why Reading People Matters

Introduction

Humans are intricate beings with distinctive thoughts, feelings, and motivations. It can be difficult to understand and decipher these aspects of people. A valuable skill in many facets of life is the capacity to read people, to recognize and decipher their nonverbal cues, verbal expressions, and underlying emotions. Reading people can greatly improve our comprehension, communication, and decision-making skills in all types of interactions, including interpersonal, professional, and social ones. This article will discuss the importance of reading people and how it can have a positive effect on various aspects of our lives.

Improved Communication

One of the main benefits of reading people is that it helps us communicate more effectively. Nonverbal cues like body language, tone of voice, and facial expressions can also be used to communicate in addition to words. We can learn more about what someone is really saying beyond what they say by observing and deciphering these cues. We can react appropriately, identify with their feelings, and develop deep connections thanks to this understanding. Consider a scenario where a friend claims to be "fine" despite their body language indicating otherwise. You can identify a person's true emotions and give them the support or assistance they need if you are aware of their nonverbal cues. We are able to close communication gaps, promote trust, and create stronger relationships thanks to our ability to read people accurately.

The Management of Emotional Dynamics

In our daily interactions, emotions are crucial because they affect our actions, choices, and interpersonal relationships. We can successfully navigate emotional dynamics when we are able to read people's emotions. We can react with empathy, compassion, and support when we are able to recognize and comprehend the emotions that others are expressing. The capacity to read emotions promotes intimacy and deeper connections in interpersonal relationships. It enables us to recognize when a loved one is unhappy, joyful, or in need of comfort, allowing us to react appropriately and offer the necessary emotional support. This ability can avoid misunderstandings, settle disputes, and strengthen interpersonal ties.

Reading people's emotions can also enhance teamwork and collaboration in professional settings. By recognizing our coworkers' emotional states, we can modify our communication methods, provide support when required, and foster a more positive and effective work environment.

Building Trust and Spotting Deception

Being able to read people becomes essential for spotting deceit and upholding trust in a world where lying is common. Nonverbal cues can often reveal important information about a person's sincerity or deception. Microexpressions, alterations in body language, and discrepancies between verbal and nonverbal cues can serve as warning signs of possible deception. We can improve our capacity to spot deception by developing our ability to read nonverbal cues from others. This ability is especially useful when determining someone else's credibility or during negotiations or job interviews. We can protect our interests, avoid potential harm, and make well-informed decisions with the aid of deception detection.Accurate people reading also promotes relationship trust. People are more likely to trust and confide in us when they believe that we understand them, their emotions, and their intentions. Healthy relationships, whether personal or professional, are built on trust, and reading people is essential to building and sustaining that trust.

Cross-Cultural Differences and Adaptation

Interactions with people from different cultural backgrounds are becoming more prevalent in today's globalized world. Cultural differences can be seen in a variety of ways, such as in expression of emotions, body language conventions, and communication methods. Effectively navigating these cross-cultural differences requires the ability to read people.

We can interpret the subtle nuances of nonverbal cues and modify our communication by cultivating cross-cultural sensitivity and understanding. This ability enables us to prevent cultural differences may lead to misinterpretations, misunderstandings, and potential conflicts. Understanding cultural norms, values, and customs, which affect how emotions are expressed and communicated, is necessary when reading people in a cross-cultural setting.

For instance, maintaining eye contact may be viewed as a sign of respect and attention in some cultures while disrespectful or confrontational in others. We can modify our own behavior and communication style to ensure successful and respectful interactions by reading people within their cultural context.

Reading people from different cultures also teaches us to value and embrace diversity. It enables us to gain a deeper comprehension of and empathy for people with various backgrounds, fostering inclusive and peaceful relationships. We can create bridges of connection and encourage cultural exchange by acknowledging and respecting cultural differences.

Making Better Decisions

Reading people well is useful in both social and personal contexts, as well as during decision-making. People's actions, nonverbal cues, and communication methods frequently reveal important details that can guide our conclusions and decisions.

In business and professional settings, for instance, reading people during discussions or meetings can reveal information about the intentions, goals, and motivations of the parties involved. Making better decisions and negotiating better agreements may be facilitated by an understanding of the underlying dynamics.

Managers can assess the needs and concerns of their team members in leadership roles by reading people. Leaders can effectively motivate and support their employees, which will increase productivity and job satisfaction, by understanding their emotions, strengths, and weaknesses.

The capacity to read people aids in risk assessment, character evaluation, and decision-making about whom to trust or interact with in various spheres of our lives. The ability to read people enables us to make choices that are consistent with our values and objectives, whether we are selecting friends, romantic partners, or business associates.

Benefits of Understanding Human Behavior

An essential component of our social and personal lives is comprehending human behavior. It enables us to move through different interactions, create deep connections, and reach wise decisions. In this article, we will examine the many advantages of learning about human behavior and enquire into the ways in which it can enhance various facets of our lives.

1. Better Communication: Having better communication skills is one of the main advantages of understanding human behavior.Understanding nonverbal cues like body language, tone of voice, and facial expressions will help us better understand what others are trying to say. This enables us to interact meaningfully and effectively by responding appropriately and changing our communication style.

2. Creating Stronger Relationships: We can better understand the wants, needs, and motives of others by understanding human behavior. We can develop empathy and a deeper understanding of other people's viewpoints thanks to this knowledge, which also helps us create more solid and sincere relationships. We can resolve disputes more skillfully, anticipate the requirements of our loved ones, and foster a friendly and peaceful social atmosphere.

3. Effective Leadership: Inspiring and motivating their teams is significantly easier for leaders who are aware of human behavior. They are able to accurately assign tasks, offer helpful support, and foster an environment that fosters productivity and individual development because they have a good sense of their team members' emotions, motivations, and strengths. Leaders can better communicate their vision and objectives by having a better understanding of human behavior, which increases employee engagement and satisfaction.

4. Conflict Resolution: Conflict occurs naturally in human interactions, but knowing how people behave gives us the skills to handle and end conflicts more skillfully. We can approach conflicts with empathy and come up with solutions if we are aware of the underlying emotions and viewpoints of those involved. Our capacity to diffuse conflict, promote candid communication, and identify points of agreement improves our ability to solve problems and leads to relationships that are healthier and more peaceful.

5. Personal Development and Self-Awareness: Learning about ourselves and our own thoughts, feelings, and behaviors is an important part of understanding human behavior. The development of the self requires this self-awareness. By identifying our own tendencies and prejudices, we can consciously choose to get around obstacles, raise our emotional quotient, and form better routines. Understanding how people behave enables us to spot our own shortcomings and take action to become the best versions of ourselves.

6. Success in Professional Environments: Success in professional settings can be greatly aided by an understanding of human behavior. The ability to read and understand people gives us a competitive edge in all areas of life, including sales, negotiations, and client relationships. We can modify our approach, customize our communication, and establish rapport with clients and coworkers by paying attention to nonverbal cues. Additionally, having this understanding enables us to successfully negotiate office politics, work together, and improve team dynamics.

7. Conflict Prevention: Understanding human behavior can help prevent conflicts in addition to resolving them. We can prevent problems from worsening by being proactive in addressing them by identifying potential triggers and sources of conflict. By creating a supportive and inclusive environment, we can lessen the likelihood of miscommunications and conflicts in the first place. This is done by understanding the needs and viewpoints of others.

8. Making Well-Informed Decisions: Having a solid understanding of how people behave helps us make well-informed decisions in both our

personal and professional lives. We can make better decisions if we take into account the motives, biases, and outside factors that affect human behavior. This information enables us to assess risks, foresee potential outcomes, and take other people's feelings into account when making decisions. Making decisions that are in line with our values and goals while taking into account the needs and expectations of those around us is made possible by our understanding of human behavior.

Ethical Considerations
Ethics-Related Matters

In every endeavor, ethics are essential, and reading people is no different. It is crucial to approach human behavior with a solid ethical foundation when trying to understand and interpret it. This chapter explores the various ethical issues raised by treating people like books and offers advice on how to use this skill in a responsible and respectful manner.

Observing personal privacy

Respecting personal privacy is one of the most important ethical issues when reading people. Insights into someone's thoughts and feelings can be gained by observing nonverbal cues and deciphering verbal cues, but it's important to keep in mind that everyone has the right to privacy. Without their consent, entering into someone's personal space or their privacy is an infringement on their autonomy and can erode relationships' trust.

When trying to read people, it is crucial to set boundaries and get permission. Be considerate of their comfort zones and respect their personal space. A person should not be bothered by intrusive questions or interrogations that may make them feel vulnerable or uncomfortable. Instead, concentrate on fostering an atmosphere of openness and trust where people feel free to voluntarily express their thoughts and emotions.

Keeping bias and stereotypes at bay

The need to avoid bias and stereotyping when reading people is another crucial ethical consideration. Humans are complex creatures with a variety of histories, life experiences, and personalities. It's crucial to acknowledge and value each person for who they are, rather than drawing conclusions or making generalizations based on a small sample of data.

It is unfair to stereotype people based on their gender, race, ethnicity, or any other characteristic, and it also feeds negative biases. It's important to approach people with an open mind, devoid of assumptions or biases. Focus on understanding people as unique beings, taking into account their particular circumstances and perspectives, rather than relying on stereotypes.

Keeping Objectivity and Refraining from Manipulation

Maintaining objectivity and avoiding manipulation are responsibilities that come along with reading people. Understanding people's behavior shouldn't be done to control or take advantage of them. Instead, the focus should be on encouraging improved empathy, connection, and communication.Instead of using the information to manipulate or control someone else's behavior, it is critical to approach reading people from a place of genuine interest in helping them understand and feeling supported. Do not exploit the information you gather to your disadvantage or the detriment of others. Always put people's autonomy and well-being first, making sure that your actions are motivated by compassion and respect.

Boundaries and Informed Consent

It's crucial to obtain consent and set up boundaries before engaging in people reading practice. People may seek assistance in understanding their emotions or behaviors in certain professional settings, such as counseling or therapy. In these circumstances, it is essential to clarify the goal.

Interpreting Body Language

Posture and Gestures

Nonverbal communication includes posture and gestures, which can reveal important details about a person's thoughts, feelings, and intentions. The subtleties of someone's body language can reveal important details about their personality, level of comfort, and even their sincerity. The significance of posture and gestures is explored in this article, along with how they function in social situations, work environments, and daily life.

Body:

1.The Influence of Posture

The way we hold and position our bodies is known as posture, and it is very important in nonverbal communication. Our posture frequently reflects our emotional state and can show signs of dominance, submission, or confidence. Someone with straight shoulders and an open stance is typically seen as self-assured and approachable, whereas someone with slumped shoulders and a closed-off stance may be trying to show disinterest or discomfort. Knowing how posture affects us gives us the ability to decipher the nonverbal cues people use to communicate.

2. Gestures: Wordless Expressions

The intentional or unintentional movements of our hands, arms, and other body parts that go along with our speech or stand alone to send messages are known as gestures. They strengthen verbal communication by adding nuance and emphasis, which improves our capacity to convey ideas, express feelings, or convey meaning. For instance, hand movements can highlight important conversational points while pointing can be used to indicate direction or draw attention to a specific object. However, gestures can also differ between cultures, so it's crucial to take cultural context into account when interpreting them.

3. Nonverbal Signals in Workplace Contexts

In professional settings, posture and gestures have a big impact on how others see us and how successful we are in our careers. In a job interview, standing straight and paying attention demonstrates professionalism and confidence, while excessive fidgeting or crossed arms could be an indication of anxiety or defensiveness. Furthermore, being aware of our body language, such as keeping appropriate hand movements and refraining from distracting behaviors, can help build credibility and promote favorable impressions.

4. Posture and Expression of Emotion

Emotional expression is closely correlated with posture and gestures. Our bodies react to various emotions by taking on particular postures and gestures. A person who is feeling confident, for instance, might stand tall with their chest out, whereas a person who is feeling defeated might slouch or display closed-off body language. As a result, communication is improved and deeper connections are made because we are better able to understand and empathize with others' emotions.

5. Considerations of Culture

Cultural norms have an impact on posture and gestures, which can vary between societies. For instance, certain cultures may place a greater emphasis on respecting one another's personal space when interacting, which may affect how far apart they prefer to be. In some cultures, gestures that are regarded as acceptable or appropriate can be offensive or misinterpreted in others. When interacting with people from different backgrounds, it's crucial to become familiar with cultural differences in posture and gestures in order to prevent miscommunications.

Hand Movements and their Significance

Nonverbal communication relies heavily on hand movements, which can convey a variety of intentions and meanings. Our hands reveal a lot about our thoughts, emotions, and attitudes through subtle gestures as well as more overt actions. Knowing the significance of hand gestures can help us communicate more effectively and improve our ability to accurately read others. In order to illuminate the complex language of our hands, this article examines various hand movements and their implications in various contexts.

I. Different Hand Motions

1. Hand gestures are deliberate movements of the hands and fingers used to express ideas or messages. These hand gestures can be figurative, emphasizing or completing spoken words, or they can be cultural, like the thumbs-up sign or the "OK" hand gesture.

2. Emblems: Often specific to a particular culture or group, emblems are hand gestures with a direct verbal translation. Examples include the universally understood meanings of the "peace" sign and the "thumbs-up" gesture.

3. Illustrators: Hand gestures that support and amplify spoken words are known as illustrators. They aid in emphasizing or elaborating on the spoken message. Using hand gestures to describe an object's size or shape while speaking is one example.

4. Adaptors: Unconscious self-touching or self-soothing behaviors that reflect an individual's internal state or discomfort are known as adaptors. An example of an adaptor is rubbing one's hands together when anxious or biting one's nails.

2. The Importance of Hand Motions

1. Cultural Variations: Hand gestures and their connotations can differ from one culture to another. In another culture, what might be considered an admirable gesture might be offensive or inappropriate. To prevent misinterpretations and misunderstandings, it is essential to become familiar with cultural norms and to comprehend the subtleties of hand movements in various settings.

2. Expressing Emotions: Our hand motions and emotions are closely related. They can demonstrate someone's degree of zeal, excitement, or frustration. Clenched fists, for instance, may be used to convey rage, whereas open, expressive hand gestures may be used to convey joy or zeal.

3. Authority and Confidence: People with authority frequently make assertive hand gestures, such as firm handshakes, stern gestures, or

open palm displays. These gestures can give off an air of confidence and authority, which can positively affect how other people see the wearer.

4. Manipulation and Deception: Hand gestures can also be used to trick or manipulate other people. People sometimes use deceptive hand gestures to mask their true feelings or intentions in certain circumstances. Recognizing differences between verbal and nonverbal cues can help detect deception by highlighting subtle hand movements.

5. Cultural Norms and Gender Differences: Hand gestures are influenced by cultural norms and gender roles. Hand gestures made by men and women may differ in their intensity, use of space, or openness. Effective cross-cultural communication can be promoted and potential biases can be reduced by being aware of these differences.

III. Understanding Hand Motions

1. Context and Congruence: It is critical to take into account the context of hand movements when interpreting them. Depending on the circumstance, the same hand gesture may have different connotations. A person's message can also be better understood by observing the overall consistency of their hand gestures, facial expressions, and verbal communication.

2. Cluster analysis can help identify patterns and clusters of behavior by examining hand movements in conjunction with other nonverbal cues. Hand gestures, facial expressions, and body postures can all be used to convey different emotions, attitudes, or intentions.

3. Individual Differences: It's crucial to understand that everyone's hand movements are different from one another. as a result of individual preferences, cultural heritages, and personality traits. While some people may move their hands more expressively than others, others might be more reserved. Accurate interpretation can be ensured by recognizing these unique individual differences, which can help prevent generalizations.

4. Baseline and Changes: To identify deviations or changes in behavior, it is essential to establish a baseline of a person's typical hand movements. Uncomfortableness, stress, or hidden emotions may be indicated by sudden changes in hand gestures, such as increased fidgeting or clenched fists.

5. Self-Awareness: It's equally crucial to become conscious of our own hand motions. By being aware of the messages our hands send, we can better understand one another and align our nonverbal cues with our intended communication.

Conclusion

In nonverbal communication, hand gestures have a significant meaning that can reveal important information about a person's thoughts, emotions, and intentions. We can improve our ability to accurately read people by learning about the various hand gestures, their cultural implications, and their significance in various situations. It takes consideration of individual differences, cultural norms, and an understanding of all of a person's nonverbal cues to interpret hand movements. By applying this knowledge to our interactions, we can improve our ability to communicate, forge stronger bonds, and handle social situations. Remember that we can learn more about those around us by deciphering the language of our hands, which is a potent tool.

Nonverbal Cues in Different Cultural Contexts
When taking into account various cultural contexts, the importance of nonverbal communication in human interactions becomes even more clear. Nonverbal cues, gestures, and expressions that express meanings and emotions are specific to each culture. Accurately understanding and interpreting these cues is crucial for successful cross-cultural communication and relationship building.

Numerous nonverbal communication cues, such as facial expressions, body language, gestures, proxemics (personal space), eye contact, and vocal tonality, show cultural differences. Let's examine a few of these nonverbal cues and how they vary depending on the cultural setting.

Facial expressions are among the most widely used nonverbal communication techniques. However, cultural interpretations of particular expressions can differ. For instance, a smile is typically indicative of friendliness or happiness. A smile, however, can also signify embarrassment or trepidation in some cultures. Similar to how some cultures view direct eye contact as a challenge or a sign of disrespect, others may view it as a sign of respect.

Body Language: Cultural differences in body language have a big impact on how people communicate messages and emotions. For instance, cultural differences can affect what a nod means. A nod may denote agreement or understanding in some cultures while merely showing attention in others. Similar variations in meaning can be found in hand gestures. In some Middle Eastern nations, the "thumbs up" gesture, which is frequently used to express approval or positivity in Western cultures, may be offensive.

Proxemics: The use and perception of personal space are referred to as proxemics. The appropriate distance between people when communicating is determined by cultural norms. People stand closer to one another and make more physical contact during conversations in some cultures, while standing further apart is preferred in others. These expectations should be followed to avoid discomfort or misunderstandings. To foster a welcoming and respectful atmosphere, it is essential to recognize and respect the cultural differences in proxemics.

Another nonverbal cue that differs significantly across cultures is eye contact. Direct eye contact is frequently interpreted in Western cultures as a sign of engagement, honesty, and attention. However, prolonged eye contact may be viewed as rude or intrusive in many Asian cultures. Avoiding eye contact with elders or other people in positions of authority is considered respectful in some African cultures. Misunderstandings or poor judgments can result from a failure to recognize eye contact cues.

Vocal Tonality: Cultural interpretations of vocal tonality vary. Different emotions and attitudes can be communicated through speech using tone, pitch, and volume. For instance, in some cultures, a loud, assertive voice may be interpreted as confident, while in others, it may come across as impolite or aggressive. Similar cultural differences can be found in how quickly people speak, with some cultures valuing clarity and emphasis over speed.

Cultural Sensitivity and Adaptability: It is crucial to approach cross-cultural communication with sensitivity and adaptability in order to successfully navigate nonverbal cues in various cultural contexts. Here are some crucial things to remember:

1. Cultural education: Get to know the nonverbal cues and accepted communication styles of the people you will be interacting with. It can be beneficial to read books, articles, or take part in cultural workshops.

2. Observation and Adaptation: Study the nonverbal cues that members of a particular culture use, and modify your own behavior accordingly. In various social settings, pay attention to cues like body language, proxemics, and facial expressions.

3. Avoiding Stereotypes: Keep in mind that there can be significant individual variations and that cultural norms are not absolute. Be careful not to generalize or stereotype people based on their cultural background.

4. Ask for Clarification: Don't be afraid to ask politely for clarification if you are unsure of the meaning of a nonverbal cue. People respect those who express an interest in learning about and respecting their cultural customs.

5. Develop Empathy: Empathy helps you comprehend and appreciate the ways that cultures differ in nonverbal communication. Consider the perspectives of others, take into account their cultural heritage, and approach interactions with an open mind and a sincere desire to learn.

6. Nonverbal Sensitivity: Active listening and observation exercises will help you become more sensitive to subtle nonverbal cues. During conversations, pay attention to the body language, vocal intonation, and facial expressions. This sensitivity will develop over time and become more instinctive.

7. Flexibility and Adaptability: Be ready to modify your nonverbal communication approach to fit the cultural situation. To ensure effective communication and rapport-building, you might need to modify your body language, gestures, and eye contact.

8. Respectful Gestures and Etiquette: Learn which gestures and mannerisms are regarded as respectful or offensive in various cultures. This covers bows, handshakes, greetings, and other nonverbal exchanges.

9. Patience and Understanding: As you navigate cultural differences in nonverbal communication, have patience with both yourself and other people. Recognize that miscommunications can happen and that developing cultural sensitivity and fluency in reading nonverbal cues takes time and practice.

10. Learn from Mistakes: Rather than dwelling on a cultural faux pas or misreading of a nonverbal cue, look at it as an opportunity to grow. Think back on the experience, get feedback if necessary, and use it to improve your ability to communicate across cultures.

You can foster effective communication, forge stronger bonds, and successfully navigate cross-cultural interactions by embracing cultural diversity and improving your understanding of nonverbal cues in various cultural contexts.

Analyzing Eye Movements and Gaze

Eye Contact and its Interpretation

Human communication is fundamentally based on eye contact, which is essential for comprehending the feelings, intentions, and thoughts of others. As they are able to reveal a wealth of information beyond verbal expressions, the eyes are frequently referred to as the windows to the soul. The importance of eye contact and how it is interpreted in social interactions, professional settings, and cultural differences will all be covered in this article. We will examine the various forms of eye contact, how it affects interpersonal relationships, and how cultural norms on eye contact vary. Knowing the subtleties of eye contact can help us read people more accurately, build relationships, and communicate more successfully.

Eye Contact Has Power

Making eye contact is a potent nonverbal cue that builds relationships and communicates ideas without using words. It is an essential part of social interaction because it can convey feelings, attention, and interest. Making eye contact with people lets them know we're listening and participating in the conversation. It fosters a sense of kinship and can strengthen relationships between people.

Eye Contact Styles

Each type of eye contact conveys a different message and can vary in duration, intensity, and purpose. Greetings or acknowledgements can be conveyed with quick glances, whereas interest, attraction, or dominance can be expressed through prolonged eye contact. On the other hand, avoiding eye contact could be a sign of shyness, deception, or disinterest. Furthermore, the angle of eye contact can reveal information. Direct eye contact, on the other hand, can convey confidence or assertiveness while averting the gaze can convey discomfort or submission.

Understanding Eye Contact in Various Situations

1. Interactions with Others: Eye contact is essential for expressing emotions and forming connections in social situations. During conversations, keeping appropriate eye contact demonstrates active listening, respect, and interest in the other person's viewpoints. However, how eye contact is perceived can vary depending on cultural norms and personal preferences. For instance, while some cultures view extended eye contact as rude or intrusive, others view it as a sign of respect and engagement.

2. Business Environments: Making eye contact in formal settings can project professionalism, assurance, and credibility. Maintaining eye contact with the interviewer during a job interview shows focus and assurance. It may denote authority and assertiveness in discussions or negotiations. Striking a balance is crucial, though, as extended or

intense eye contact could be interpreted as aggressive or confrontational.

3. Romantic Relationships: Eye contact is important in romantic relationships because it can elicit strong emotions and intimacy. The emotional connection and understanding between romantic partners can be improved by maintaining eye contact. It may also denote desire and attraction. Eye contact can mean different things to different people, so it's important to take your comfort level and personal preferences into account.

4. Cultural Variations: If cultural differences are not understood, misinterpretations may occur because eye contact norms vary across cultures. Direct eye contact may be regarded as rude or challenging in some cultures, where it is expected and represents honesty and respect. Understanding these cultural differences can reduce miscommunication and promote effective cross-cultural interaction.

Eye Movements and Cognitive Processes

Our ability to perceive and interact with the world around us depends heavily on our ability to move our eyes. Research has shown that eye movements are closely linked to cognitive processes like perception, attention, memory, and decision-making in addition to serving the basic purpose of directing visual attention. The intriguing connection between eye movements and cognitive functions is explored in this article, along with the underlying mechanisms and implications for comprehending human cognition.

1. Visual Perception and Eye Movements: Visual perception starts with the eyes capturing visual data, which the brain then processes. Eye movements are a way for the brain to actively explore the visual scene by focusing the gaze on significant details and interesting objects. Studies have shown that specific eye movements, such as fixations and saccades, are closely related to the perceptual procedures involved in scene understanding, spatial awareness, and object recognition.

2. Attentional Control and Eye Movements: Attention is a fundamental cognitive process that allows us to narrow our attention to the information that is important to us while excluding irrelevant

information. As we naturally direct our gaze to things or areas that catch our attention, eye movements serve as a physical representation of attentional control. Our capacity to process and organize visual stimuli is improved by the effective allocation of cognitive resources made possible by the coordination between attention and eye movements.

3. Memory Encoding and Retrieval: The processes of memory encoding and retrieval are also influenced by eye movements. The areas we fixate on while actively exploring a visual scene with our gaze are more likely to be remembered than the surrounding areas. This phenomenon, also referred to as "eye movement-based memory effects," emphasizes how important eye movements are for improving memory. Additionally, studies have shown that by reenacting the eye movement patterns seen during encoding, eye movements during retrieval can aid memory retrieval.

4. Making Decisions and Eye Movements:

Eye movements offer important insights into the cognitive processes that underlie decisions in the area of decision-making. Different tactics and biases have been discovered by examining eye movement patterns during tasks involving perceptual judgments, risk assessment, and information processing. Eye movements, for instance, can reveal attentional biases toward particular options, affect how alternatives are evaluated, and show how visual information is incorporated during decision-making.

5. Cognitive Disorders and Eye Movements: Abnormal eye movements have been seen in a number of cognitive disorders, providing insight into the underlying mechanisms of these conditions. As an illustration, those who suffer from attention deficit hyperactivity disorder (ADHD) frequently have increased saccadic eye movements and struggle to restrain inappropriate eye movements. The understanding and diagnosis of neurological disorders like Parkinson's disease, Alzheimer's disease, and schizophrenia have benefited from the study of eye movements.

6. Technological Applications: The connection between eye movements and cognitive functions has made way for a variety of

technological uses. Application areas for eye-tracking technology include user interface design, market research, psychology, and neuroscience. It records and analyzes eye movements. Insights into human behavior, attentional patterns, and cognitive workload are gained, which helps researchers and practitioners create more logical and effective systems.

Researchers have also been able to delve deeper into the complex relationship between eye movements and cognitive processes as a result of recent developments in eye-tracking technology. It is now possible to analyze eye movement patterns and their effects on cognition in greater detail thanks to high-resolution eye trackers with better precision and sampling rates. These developments have opened up fresh research directions and hold the promise of advancing our knowledge of human cognition.

The function of eye movements in reading and language processing is one area of ongoing research. Eye movements reveal important details about how we decipher written text, focus our attention on particular words or phrases, and understand the meaning of sentences. Researchers can study a variety of aspects of language processing, including word recognition, syntactic parsing, and semantic integration, by monitoring eye movements while subjects read.

Eye movements have also been investigated in relation to the development of expertise and skills. Experts in particular fields, like chess players or professional athletes, exhibit different eye movement patterns from beginners. These patterns demonstrate their capacity to quickly decide based on their knowledge and process pertinent information in an effective manner. Researchers want to understand the cognitive processes that underlie expert eye movements in order to develop training and skill-building strategies.

Additionally, eye movements are very important for social interaction and communication. According to studies, when people are speaking face-to-face, they maintain eye contact with one another while engaging in mutual gaze. Mutual gaze is connected to a number of social and cognitive functions, such as empathy, rapport-building, and attention. On the other hand, departures from typical gaze patterns may point to social challenges or specific mental illnesses, such as autism spectrum disorder.

Research on eye movements and cognitive processes has also benefited the field of human-computer interaction. Designers can optimize the positioning of crucial elements and enhance user experience by looking at where users look when interacting with interfaces. Eye-tracking data can offer insightful information about users' attentional patterns, visual preferences, and cognitive workload, ultimately resulting in the creation of interfaces that are more understandable and user-friendly.

It is important to remember that while eye movements can reveal important details about cognitive processes, they do not necessarily correspond to internal mental states. Numerous elements, such as task demands, environmental stimuli, and individual differences, have an impact on eye movements. Because of this, care must be taken when interpreting eye movement data, and results should be taken into account in conjunction with other measurements and contextual data.

Detecting Signs of Honesty or Deception through Gaze

A fascinating area of research examines the relationship between eye movements and people's sincerity and identifies telltale signs of honesty or deception. The eyes are frequently referred to as the "windows to the soul," as they can reveal a great deal about a person's internal state and intentions. This article explores the science of eye movement reading to find potential signs of sincerity or deception. Understanding the subtleties of gaze patterns and how to interpret them can help people improve their ability to judge the truthfulness of others, which will help them communicate more effectively and make better decisions.

I. How Eye Contact Is Important

Eye contact is crucial for effective interpersonal communication and is frequently linked to sincerity and reliability. When someone makes steady eye contact, it conveys assurance and openness and may even be a sign of sincerity. However, avoiding eye contact or not making eye contact at all could indicate deception. This section examines the significance of eye contact and how it affects how honesty is perceived.

II. Deception and Gaze Aversion

Direct eye contact avoidance, or gaze aversion, is frequently linked to dishonest behavior. Even though it is not a surefire sign of dishonesty, it can be a potential warning sign. The psychological bases of gaze aversion and its relationship to dishonest intentions are examined in this section. It also emphasizes how crucial it is to take cultural and contextual considerations into account when interpreting gaze aversion.

III. Cognitive Processes and Eye Movements

Eye movements can reveal information about a person's thought processes and reveal whether they are being honest or lying. Certain eye movements, such as quick or prolonged blinking, staring in a particular direction, or dilated pupils, have been shown in studies to be signs of underlying cognitive and emotional processes connected to deception. The relationship between eye movements and cognitive functions is explored in this section, along with any potential indications of honesty or deception they may contain.

IV. Eye Movements and Microexpressions

Microexpressions are brief, unintentional facial movements that can reveal important details about a person's true emotions. Microexpressions, when paired with eye gaze patterns, can reveal a person's sincerity or deception. This section examines the relationship between microexpressions and eye gaze, emphasizing how determining sincerity can be aided by examining the length and direction of eye movements.

V. The Impact of Emotional Arousal

Eye gaze patterns can be significantly affected by emotional arousal, which can also signal sincerity or deception. People's gaze patterns may alter when they are feeling intense emotions like fear, anxiety, or excitement. The effect of emotional arousal on eye gaze is examined in this section, along with how careful observation can help distinguish between true emotional responses and deceptive ones.

VI. The Value of Baseline Behavior and Context

Setting up a baseline of behavior for comparison and taking into account the context are both necessary for correctly interpreting eye gaze patterns. People's eye movements can differ depending on their cultural upbringing, character traits, and unique quirks. In order to effectively identify telltale signs of honesty or deception, this section emphasizes the significance of contextual understanding and the necessity of establishing a person's typical eye gaze behavior.,

Reading People in Different Contexts

Personal Relationships
The Secret to Contentment and Happiness

The foundation of human existence is interpersonal relationships, which give us love, support, and a sense of community. They are essential in determining our overall happiness and emotional health. Our relationships, whether they be with family, friends, or romantic partners, have a significant impact on both our mental and physical health. We will examine the significance of interpersonal connections, the forces that shape them, and practical methods for fostering and preserving strong bonds in this in-depth investigation. A more contented and richer life can result from understanding and fostering meaningful relationships.

The Importance of Personal Connections

1. Relationships' Psychological Effects

Our mental and emotional well-being are significantly impacted by our interpersonal relationships. Reliable relationships help people feel less stressed, more confident, and more satisfied with their lives as a whole. On the other hand, unhealthy relationships can cause emotional distress such as anxiety and depression. It gives us the ability to create nourishing and supportive relationships when we are aware of the psychological effects of our interactions with others.

The Function of Social Support

A crucial component of interpersonal relationships is social support. The existence of a supportive network, whether it be emotional, practical, or informational support, can aid people in dealing more resolutely with life's difficulties. We will investigate the various types of social support and how they support personal growth and development.

3. How Personal Connections Affect Physical Health

The strength of interpersonal connections has been found to have a direct impact on physical health. Longer life expectancy and a lower risk of chronic diseases are linked to strong social ties. We'll look at the underlying processes that link interpersonal connections to physical health as well as the implications for medical treatment and preventative measures.

Personal Relationship Types

1. Relationships with family

One of the most important relationships in our lives is our family. We will examine how different family structures function, the value of communication, conflict resolution, and creating a nurturing home environment.

2. Companionship

Friendships are essential for social and emotional growth. It will be easier for people to form meaningful connections if they are aware of the various kinds of friendships, the characteristics of healthy friendships, and the advantages they offer.

3. Romantic Connections

Intimacy and complexity are unusual features of romantic relationships. We'll talk about how to maintain passion and commitment, how to effectively communicate, the stages of romantic relationships, and how to deal with difficulties and conflicts.

Taking Care of Your Relationships

1. Good Communications

Any healthy relationship is built on effective communication. We'll talk about conflict-resolution techniques, assertive ways to express feelings and needs, and active listening.

2. Developing Intimacy and Trust

All relationships are built on trust, and emotional closeness requires developing intimacy. We'll talk about building trust in relationships, dealing with mistrust, and developing intimacy.

3. Emotional intelligence and sympathyThe capacity for empathy is the capacity to comprehend and experience others' emotions. The ability to recognize, comprehend, and manage our own emotions as well as those of those around us is known as emotional intelligence. We'll look at how emotional acuity and empathy support happier and more fulfilling relationships.

4. Distinctiveness and Boundaries

Boundaries must be established and upheld in order to maintain healthy relationships. We'll talk about the value of uniqueness in relationships and how to strike a balance between individuality and togetherness.

Relationship issues in the personal sphere

1.Communication Mistakes

Conflicts and misunderstandings can result from poor communication and communication barriers. We will look at typical problems with communication and practical solutions.

2. Resolution of Conflict

Conflict arises in every relationship. Developing stronger relationships and preventing conflict escalation are two benefits of learning effective conflict resolution methods.

3. Handling Relationships

That Are Toxic Remove oneself from such relationships by establishing boundaries, getting help, and placing self-care first.

4. Handling Transitions in Life

Relationships can be strained by life transitions like moving, changing careers, or starting a family. We will look at methods for enduring strong connections and navigating these transitions successfully.

5. Keeping Distance Relationships Alive

Long-distance relationships have particular difficulties, but with the right strategy, they can succeed. We will talk about ways to build trust, maintain an emotional connection despite physical distance, and effective communication strategies.

6. Keeping Interdependence and Independence in Check

In interpersonal relationships, striking a healthy balance between independence and interdependence is crucial. We'll go into detail about how crucial it is to preserve individuality while promoting community.

Our personal relationships are the foundation of our lives, determining our level of satisfaction, emotional health, and overall happiness. Greater fulfillment and contentment can result from actively fostering these relationships and realizing their importance. People can develop and maintain strong and healthy relationships by using effective communication techniques, establishing trust, encouraging empathy, and overcoming obstacles with resiliency. A lifelong journey that yields enormous rewards and contributes to a happier, healthier, and more fulfilling existence is investing in personal relationships.

Understanding Nonverbal Signals in Intimate Relationships

Recognizing Nonverbal Cues in Close Relationships

The foundation of intimate relationships is one of communication, understanding, and trust. While verbal communication is essential for expressing feelings and thoughts, nonverbal cues frequently carry a deeper meaning and have a significant impact on relationship dynamics. This article will discuss the value of comprehending nonverbal cues in close relationships and how they can strengthen a couple's connection. Numerous cues, such as body language, facial expressions, touch, and tone of voice, are included in nonverbal communication. These signs can sometimes be even more telling than words about someone's feelings, goals, and intentions. Being aware of these nonverbal cues can help partners in a close relationship communicate more effectively, resolve issues, and strengthen their emotional connection.

Body language is a crucial component of nonverbal communication in close relationships. People's body positions, gestures, and physical proximity to one another can all convey a wealth of information. Crossed arms and a tense posture, for instance, may be a sign of defensiveness or discomfort, whereas open arms and a relaxed stance may indicate receptivity and comfort. When partners are aware of these cues, they can respond sympathetically and modify their behavior to promote a more harmonious relationship.

Additionally, facial expressions are very important in nonverbal communication in close relationships. The face is very expressive and can convey a wide range of emotions, including happiness and love as well as sadness or anger. Knowing how to respond empathetically to these expressions can help partners assess each other's emotional states. Furrowed brows may indicate worry or distress, while a warm smile can imply love and happiness. Partners can address emotional needs and offer comfort and support as needed by closely observing these facial cues.

Another potent nonverbal cue in close relationships is touch. Physical contact between partners can be used to express love, affection, and desire while also strengthening their emotional connection. An intimate touch, a warm embrace, or holding hands can evoke feelings of closeness and intimacy. But it's important to recognize that everyone has different comfort levels with physical contact and to respect each other's boundaries. To maintain a healthy balance of touch in a relationship, effective communication about preferences and consent is essential.

Another important aspect of nonverbal communication is voice tone. There are many different emotions and attitudes that can be expressed through speech. In contrast to a harsh tone, which might be used to express frustration or anger, a soft and soothing tone can convey care and tenderness. A more loving and supportive environment can be created by partners who are aware of these subtleties, which will improve communication and understanding.

Understanding nonverbal cues in close relationships extends beyond identifying specific cues. It also entails keeping an eye out for trends and collections of nonverbal behaviors. For example, a partner may be acting distant or disconnected if they consistently avoid eye contact and display closed-off body language. On the other hand, a partner who consistently demands physical closeness and exhibits gratifying nonverbal behaviors is probably desiring more intimacy. Partners can address underlying issues and cooperate to fortify their bond by deciphering these patterns.

It is crucial to remember that deciphering nonverbal cues is not a precise science. The interpretation of these cues can be influenced by context, culture, and individual differences. What one culture might interpret as a loving gesture may be seen differently in another. For this reason, clear and honest communication is essential to ensure understanding and prevent misunderstandings.

Couples can engage in activities that foster awareness and empathy to better understand nonverbal cues in close relationships. A deeper connection can be cultivated by engaging in active listening, which involves giving each other undivided attention and responding both verbally and nonverbally. Pairs can they take turns expressing their emotions solely through nonverbal cues during activities like role-playing. With the aid of this activity, partners can improve their awareness of one another's nonverbal cues and understanding of one another.

Couples can also make a point of observing and talking about nonverbal cues during normal interactions. They can allot some time to think about their own and their partner's body language, facial expressions, and voice tones. Open, nonjudgmental discussions about nonverbal cues can help partners better comprehend one another's needs and feelings.

It's important to note that nonverbal communication isn't always simple. People occasionally unintentionally give conflicting nonverbal cues or send mixed signals. Instead of making snap judgments in such circumstances, it is crucial to approach the situation with empathy and curiosity. Partners can have an honest conversation to clear up any misunderstandings by gently inquiring about the underlying feelings or thoughts that underlie the conflicting signals.

Nonverbal cues can also serve as predictors of relational dynamics and potential problems in close relationships. For instance, abrupt alterations in nonverbal behavior like increased tension, avoidance, or decreased physical affection may point to underlying conflicts or dissatisfaction. Couples can prevent minor issues from growing into larger ones and preserve a strong and enduring relationship by being aware of these shifts and taking proactive measures to address them.

Understanding nonverbal cues in intimate relationships requires more than just reading the other person's body language; it also requires being aware of and in control of one's own nonverbal behavior. Everybody in a relationship brings their own set of nonverbal communication habits and styles. Self-awareness and personal development can be facilitated by reflecting on one's own patterns and being receptive to feedback from the partner. It enables people to match their nonverbal cues to their true intentions and feelings, promoting relationship authenticity and trust.

In conclusion, nonverbal cues are crucial in intimate relationships because they shed light on feelings, desires, and relationship dynamics. Communication, empathy, and understanding between partners can all be improved by being aware of one another's body language, facial expressions, touch, and voice tones. Couples can strengthen their connection, deal with underlying issues, and forge a nurturing and fulfilling relationship by actively observing and talking about nonverbal cues. In order to build a strong foundation for a healthy and successful intimate relationship, keep in mind that effective nonverbal communication works in tandem with honest and open verbal communication.

Navigating Conflict and Emotional Dynamics

Human interaction inevitably involves conflict. Differences in opinions, values, or needs can lead to conflict in any setting, including interpersonal relationships, the workplace, or social gatherings.Conflict frequently results in heightened emotions, which makes things more difficult. Maintaining healthy relationships and fostering effective communication require the ability to navigate conflict and comprehend the underlying emotional dynamics.

Emotions and conflict are closely related. Different emotions, including rage, frustration, sadness, fear, and even guilt, may surface during a conflict. Our behavior, manner of speaking, and capacity for making decisions can all be impacted by these emotions. For conflicts to be resolved constructively, it is crucial to recognize and control these emotions.

Developing self-awareness is the first step in navigating conflict and emotional dynamics. Understanding our own feelings, reactions, and biases enables us to approach disagreements with more clarity and objectivity. It is critical to understand how our feelings can affect how we interpret the circumstances and how the other party behaves. We can better understand our own responses and make better decisions if we acknowledge our feelings and step back to think about them.

Another essential skill for navigating conflict and emotional dynamics is active listening. It entails listening to what is being said as well as comprehending the underlying emotions and needs being communicated. It is critical to establish a secure environment for direct and honest communication when conflicts arise. We can defuse the conflict's emotionally charged atmosphere by showing respect and empathy for the other person by actively listening to their point of view.

Understanding and controlling emotional dynamics during conflicts depends heavily on empathy. Empathy entails putting oneself in another person's position and making an effort to comprehend their needs, wants, and viewpoints. By displaying empathy, we foster an atmosphere of mutual respect and trust, which can facilitate more efficient conflict resolution. Through empathy, we can express our sincere concern for the other person's welfare and validate their feelings.

Emotional control must be maintained throughout conflicts. The capacity to manage and control one's emotions, even under trying circumstances, is referred to as emotional regulation. It is simple to let our emotions take control and act impulsively when disputes get heated. Impulsive responses, however, frequently cause the conflict to worsen. We can maintain a calm and collected demeanor, allowing us to think more clearly and rationally, by practicing emotional regulation techniques like deep breathing, pausing, or using positive self-talk.

An effective method for navigating conflict and emotional dynamics is collaborative problem-solving. Collaborative problem-solving focuses on identifying win-win solutions to conflicts rather than seeing conflicts as lose-lose situations. All parties are encouraged to actively participate in the resolution process through this method, which fosters a feeling of empowerment and ownership over the procedure. Conflicts can be turned into opportunities for growth and strengthened relationships by working together to identify shared goals and brainstorm potential solutions.

It is crucial to understand that resolving disputes does not always happen right away. It may be necessary to give some disputes some breathing room so that everyone can gather their thoughts and emotions. When dealing with conflict and emotional dynamics, patience and persistence are essential. It's critical to keep working toward a solution that considers the requirements and feelings of all parties.

Maintaining healthy relationships and effective communication requires the complex yet essential ability of navigating conflict and emotional dynamics. Conflicts can be turned into chances for growth and consolidated relationships by increasing self-awareness, practicing active listening, exhibiting empathy, maintaining emotional control, and using a collaborative problem-solving strategy. Although conflict is a natural part of human interaction, it can be handled in a way that promotes understanding, development, and connection with the right knowledge and attitude.

Furthermore, navigating conflict and emotional dynamics requires an understanding of the role that power dynamics play. Power disparities have a big effect on the emotions and how a conflict plays out. It's critical to be aware of any power imbalances that may exist during a conflict and to make sure that everyone involved feels heard and respected.

It is essential to stay away from personal attacks and concentrate on the current problem when handling conflicts. Personal insults can intensify feelings and prevent effective communication. Instead, it is advantageous to communicate your needs and concerns in a non-confrontational way by using "I" statements to discuss how the conflict has affected you personally. Finding common ground and moving toward a solution are made simpler by concentrating on the problem rather than criticizing the other person.

Finding a middle ground and being willing to compromise are also necessary for conflict resolution. While it is unlikely that all of the needs of both parties will be met, compromises that at least partially satisfy each party can be reached by looking for points of agreement and considering original ideas. This necessitates a readiness to set aside rigid viewpoints and give the relationship's harmony and general wellbeing top priority.

It may be helpful in some circumstances to seek the advice of an impartial third party, such as a mediator or counselor. A mediator can assist in fostering communication, fostering empathy, and assisting the parties in coming to amicable agreements. Their unbiased viewpoint can assist in removing obstacles and calming tense emotions.

It is crucial to engage in post-conflict reflection and learning after a conflict has been resolved. Insights for preventing future conflicts can be gained by reflecting on the conflict, the emotions involved, and the resolution procedure. We can develop our conflict-resolution abilities and stop similar conflicts from happening in the future by learning from our past mistakes.

It is significant to remember that not all disputes can be settled. Conflicts can occasionally be ongoing or involve insurmountable differences. It might be necessary in these circumstances to accept that the conflict cannot be fully resolved and instead concentrate on managing it in a way that reduces harm and upholds a certain level of functional coexistence.

The process of navigating emotional dynamics and conflict calls for constant practice and effort. Through self-reflection, learning from experiences, and getting feedback from others, it is a skill that can be honed over time. People can improve their ability to handle conflicts, create healthier relationships, and encourage clear communication by developing these skills dealing with conflict and emotional dynamics requires a variety of skills, including self-awareness, active listening, empathy, emotional regulation, group problem-solving, and knowledge of power dynamics. Individuals can navigate conflicts in a way that fosters comprehension, resolution, and personal development by using these principles and strategies. When handled properly, conflict can provide an opportunity to deepen bonds and promote transformation.

Building Trust and Deepening Connections

Establishing meaningful connections, whether in personal or professional contexts, requires developing trust and strengthening bonds. Relationships can only flourish when there is mutual respect, open communication, and emotional closeness. Trust must be earned through consistent behavior, authenticity, and vulnerability; it is not something that is given to you. The importance of trust in relationships is discussed in this article, which also offers insightful tips and practical advice on how to develop trust and strengthen interpersonal relationships.

I. How Critical Trust Is in Relationships

A. Establishing Trust

   1. The foundation of wholesome relationships is trust.

   2. Recognizing the multifaceted nature of trust

B. Advantages of Relationship Trust

   1. Increased emotional intimacy and vulnerability

   2. Improved communication and problem-solving

3. Improved cooperation and teamwork

2. Establishing Trust

A. Self-Trust Is The Basis

   1. Increasing self-awareness and self-confidence

   2. Upholding obligations and promoting personal development

   3. Exhibiting authenticity and morality

B. Trust-Inspiring Actions

   1. Reliability and consistency

   3. Transparency and openness 2. Active listening and empathy

   4. Ownership and Accountability

   5. Respect and Comprehension

C. Resolving Issues with Trust and Rebuilding Trust

   1.addressing past betrayals and seeking forgiveness;

   2. communicating with one another; and reestablishing transparency

   3. Be patient and work to create a secure environment

III. Strengthening Relationships

A Strong Emotional Bond

   1. Fostering empathy and comprehension;

   2. Sharing vulnerabilities and establishing a safe environment

   3. Emotional sensitivity and approval

B. Active Engagement and Communication

1. Powerful communication methods

2. Recognizing diversity and looking for common ground

3. Strengthening and valuing the viewpoint of the other person

Construction of Shared Experiences

1. Making happy memories

2. Participating in shared interests and activities

3. fostering a sense of connection and belonging

IV. Obstacles and Solutions

A. Establishing Trust in Business Relationships

1. Establishing trustworthiness and proficiency

2. Define boundaries and expectations clearly

3. encouraging candid and open criticism

B. Dealing with Problems of Trust in Personal Relationships

1. Forgiveness and mending of past wrongs

2. Rebuilding of trust through consistent behavior

3. Whenever necessary, obtaining expert assistance

C. Considerations Related to Culture and Relationships

Building trust requires:

1. recognizing cultural differences;

2. bridging cultural divides and advancing inclusivity

3. Modifying communication techniques to boost trust

V. Upholding Connections and Retaining Trust

A. Reliability and Consistency

    1. Upholding commitments and following through

    2. Accepting responsibility for deeds and words

    3. Establishing a track record of dependability

B. Conflict Resolution and Communication

    1. Honest and open dialogue

    2. During conflicts, active listening and empathy

    3. Looking for solutions that benefit both parties

C. Expressing gratitude and appreciation

    1. Giving thanks for the other person,

    2.recognizing their contributions, and expressing your gratitude for them

    3. Miniature acts of generosity and consideration

D. Adjusting to Growth and Change

    1. Accepting personal and interpersonal development

    2. Modifying standards and encouraging each other's growth by being adaptable and open-minded

6. Connectivity and Trust in the Digital Age

A. Creating Online Credibility

1. Online transparency and authenticity

2. Factors relating to privacy and data security

3. Using digital communication to establish rapport and connection

B. Promoting Online Relationships

1. Participation in active online communities

2. Using technology to foster meaningful relationships

3. Keeping offline and online interactions in check

C. Overcoming Online Challenges and Misunderstandings

1. Effective communication in online settings

2. Proactively resolving disputes and misunderstandings

3. Increasing trust in virtual and remote teams

7. The Function of Self-Care in Developing Relationships and Trust

A Foundation for Healthy Relationships is Self-Care

1. Setting self-care as a top priority to maintain emotional health and caring for   personal needs

2. Increasing awareness of oneself and introspection

B. Increasing Self-Trust to Increase Trust

1. Upholding one's moral principles and integrity

2. Growing in self-awareness and compassion

3. Being genuine and open with oneself

C. Seeking Opportunities for Growth and Support

    1. Establishing a support system for personal growth

    2. Getting counseling or coaching when necessary

    3. Supporting lifelong learning and personal development

Trust-building and relationship-deepening are ongoing processes that call for effort, empathy, and self-reflection. Although trust is brittle, it can grow and become more profound over time with consistent behavior, effective communication, and respect for one another. People can establish and maintain meaningful relationships in both the personal and professional spheres by fostering emotional connections, overcoming obstacles, and engaging in self-care. In addition to enhancing our lives, developing trust and stronger relationships also has a positive knock-on effect that promotes healthier societies and a more interconnected world. Let's embrace the process of developing trust and closer ties because it is only through these ties that we can truly appreciate and find fulfillment in human relationships.

Ethical and Responsible Application
Using Your Skills Responsibly

It is imperative to stress the responsible and ethical use of these skills in a world where the capacity to read people can offer significant advantages. It is important to always approach understanding other people and interpreting their behavior with caution, respect, and a commitment to acting responsibly. This article aims to offer advice on how to employ your ability to read people in a responsible and ethical manner, ensuring favorable results for all parties concerned.

1. Awareness of Intentions: It's important to consider your intentions before using your ability to read people. Why do you want a better understanding of others? Do you want to strengthen your relationships, communicate more effectively, or demonstrate more empathy? Your actions will be guided by a clear and moral purpose, which will also guard against the potential abuse of your skills.

2. Respect for Privacy: To use your skills responsibly, you must have a strong regard for others' privacy. It is important to realize that not everyone wants their thoughts, feelings, or intentions to be understood by others. Recognize the physical and psychological limits of personal space. Avoid prying into people's personal affairs or taking advantage of their weaknesses for your own gain. Building trust and preserving healthy relationships require respect for privacy.

3. Consent and Boundaries: When trying to read someone, getting their consent should always come first. Asking permission allows them to choose whether they feel comfortable with you interpreting their behavior while also demonstrating respect for their autonomy. To make the other person feel safe and understood, communicate openly and set clear boundaries.

4. Empathy and Compassion: It's crucial to approach people reading with empathy and compassion. Keep in mind that every person is different, having their own experiences, feelings, and difficulties. With the help of empathy, you can relate to people more deeply and

comprehend their viewpoints without passing judgment. You can foster an environment of trust and support by displaying compassion.

5. Nonjudgmental Attitude: Using a nonjudgmental attitude is a responsible way to read people. Avoid jumping to conclusions or making hasty judgments based on scant evidence. Instead, keep an open mind and take into account all of the potential influences on behavior. Recognize that a wide range of internal and external factors can have an impact on human behavior.

6. Cultural Sensitivity: Because different cultures have different norms, gestures, and expressions, cultural sensitivity is essential when reading people. Be aware of cultural variations and refrain from assuming things based on your own culture. Learn about various cultural practices to prevent misunderstandings and wrong interpretations.

7. Avoid Manipulation: Using your skills responsibly means never taking advantage of or manipulating others. The ability to read people should be utilized to create sincere bonds, enable efficient communication, and promote comprehension. Manipulative methods damage people and relationships by eroding trust. Put your skills to work fostering constructive interactions and personal development.

8. Recognizing Bias: It's critical to be aware of your own biases when interpreting others. Biases can skew how you interpret other people's actions and result in erroneous judgments. Examine your own beliefs and biases on a regular basis, actively challenging and enlarging your perspectives. Developing self-awareness enables you to make decisions that are more unbiased and just.

9. Continuous Learning and Improvement: To use your skills responsibly, you must constantly learn new things and work on yourself. To improve your comprehension of human behavior, keep up with the latest psychological research, cultural understanding, and research. Ask for input from dependable people who can help you improve your strategy and offer constructive criticism. Be a responsible reader of people who always strives for moral behavior and personal development.

Respecting Privacy Boundaries

A crucial component of interpersonal interactions and ethical communication is observing privacy boundaries. A fundamental human right, privacy gives people autonomy and control over their own private information, ideas, and experiences. Understanding and upholding privacy boundaries is even more important in this digital age, where personal information is readily available. This essay will examine the value of upholding privacy boundaries, go over various situations where privacy may be jeopardized, and offer helpful advice for making sure privacy is upheld in various situations.

I. The Value of Adhering to Privacy Boundaries

1. Individual Freedom and Autonomy: Respecting privacy boundaries recognizes and upholds a person's autonomy and their right to decide whether or not to share personal information. Individuals are empowered to maintain a sense of control and personal freedom because it gives them the opportunity to define their boundaries and decide which aspects of their lives they want to keep private.

2. Trust and Relationship Building: It's crucial to respect privacy boundaries in order to establish and uphold relationships based on trust. People are more likely to open up and share private experiences, thoughts, and emotions if they feel that their privacy is respected. This encourages closer ties and raises relationships' general level of quality.

3. Emotional Well-being: Maintaining privacy boundaries gives people a safe place to express their feelings without worrying about being

judged or bothered. This promotes emotional well-being. It enables self-improvement, introspection, and the growth of a solid sense of self.

II. Situations in which Privacy Boundaries May Be Violated:

1. Online privacy: In the digital age, it is simple to access, share, or use someone else's personal information without their permission. Data breaches, social media, and online platforms all pose serious privacy risks. To protect personal information, it is essential to be aware of the risks and take the necessary precautions.

2. Workplace Privacy: Maintaining a professional atmosphere that values people's privacy and confidentiality requires that workplace privacy boundaries be respected. Invasion of privacy at work can result in a loss of trust, lessening of job satisfaction, and even legal repercussions.

3. Intimate Relationships: Recognizing and respecting personal space, individual preferences, and the need for confidentiality are all part of respecting privacy boundaries in intimate relationships. In these kinds of relationships, crossing privacy boundaries can result in a loss of trust, emotional distress, and possible relationship dissolution.

III. Recommendations for Upholding Privacy Boundaries:

1. Consent and Communication: Ask for permission before disclosing personal information or starting a conversation that might include delicate subjects. Setting and upholding privacy boundaries requires open and honest communication.

2. Confidentiality: Uphold the privacy of any personal information given to you. Never discuss another person's private matters without that person's express consent.

3. Online Privacy Measures: Be proactive in protecting your online privacy by using strong passwords, enabling two-factor authentication, being cautious about the information you share on social media, and routinely checking your privacy settings.

4. Workplace Policies and Procedures: Become familiar with the workplace's confidentiality and privacy policies. Be cautious when handling sensitive information and respect the restrictions imposed by these policies.

5. Empathy and Sensitivity: Use empathy and sensitivity when talking about sensitive issues. Approach conversations with care and consideration, keeping in mind the emotional impact your words or actions may have on others.

6. Establish and maintain open communication about privacy boundaries in intimate relationships. 6. Boundaries in Intimate Relationships. Talk to your partner about what information can be shared with others and what information should be kept private.

The Difficulties of Respecting Privacy Boundaries

1. Cultural differences: Different cultures have different views on privacy; what one culture may consider private, another may view as more public. Cultural sensitivity and observance of various privacy norms are crucial.

2. Technology and Surveillance: The quick development of technology has created fresh problems for privacy. Privacy invasion worries are stoked by surveillance cameras, data collection procedures, and how

widely used online tracking is. It is crucial to fight for more robust privacy protections and educate oneself on how to use technology safely and responsibly.

3. Social Norms and Peer Pressure: Social norms and peer pressure can occasionally encourage people to gossip or share too much personal information. Even in social situations, it is imperative to have the courage to uphold personal boundaries and respect others' privacy.

4. Maintaining a Balance Between Transparency and Privacy: Transparency and open communication are valuable, even though privacy is crucial. In order to strike a balance between openness and privacy, careful thought and a shared understanding of appropriate boundaries are required.

Respecting privacy restrictions is a crucial component of moral communication and fulfilling relationships. It promotes trust, respects people's autonomy, and aids in emotional health. It is crucial to be watchful and proactive in protecting and respecting privacy in a time when personal information is readily available and technology frequently puts privacy at risk. We can build a society that values and upholds privacy rights by asking for consent, maintaining confidentiality, being aware of online privacy, and being sensitive to cultural differences. Let's work to create a society that values empathy, respect, and appropriate behavior when it comes to personal space, which will ultimately lead to deeper and more fulfilling relationships.

Avoiding Misinterpretations and Assumptions

Misunderstandings, disputes, and strained relationships can result from assumptions and misinterpretations. It's critical to reduce these blunders when reading people in order to fully comprehend other people and their intentions. This chapter looks at how to navigate social situations more skillfully by avoiding misunderstandings and presumptions.

1. The Dangers of Inaccuracies and Assumptions

Misinterpretations happen when we give someone's words, actions, or body language the wrong meaning. On the other hand, assumptions are the beliefs or decisions we make without enough data or information. Biases, a narrow perspective, or insufficient information can lead to both misinterpretations and assumptions. They may impair our capacity for accurate people reading and result in incorrect inferences.

2. Grow your own awareness

The key to avoiding misunderstandings and presumptions is self-awareness. You can avoid being influenced by others' interpretations of you by being aware of your own biases, preconceptions, and triggers. You can approach interactions with a more open mind and a willingness to ask questions rather than making snap judgments if you are aware of your own limitations.

3. Use active listening techniques

Giving the speaker your full attention and trying to understand their point of view are both parts of active listening. Instead of assuming what the other person is trying to say, pay attention to their words, tone, and nonverbal cues. To make sure you understand their intended meaning, paraphrase or summarize their message. You can avoid misunderstandings and get a more precise understanding of the other person's thoughts and feelings by actively listening.

4. Look for Details

When in doubt, it is imperative to get more information rather than assuming. Ask for more information if you are unclear about the meaning of someone's words or behavior. Avoid assuming what they intend or drawing conclusions without enough information. Clarifying information can promote better communication and help clear up misunderstandings.

5. Take Cultural Differences and Context into Account

Failure to take into account the context or cultural variances that may affect someone's behavior frequently leads to misinterpretations.

Individuals' modes of expression can be influenced by the norms, values, and communication practices of their respective cultures. Consider the cultural background of the person you are speaking to and be aware of any potential differences in nonverbal cues, personal space, and communication style.

6. Validate and Identify with

Work to understand and validate others in order to prevent misunderstandings. You can show that you respect someone's viewpoint and acknowledge their feelings or experiences by validating them. Empathy enables you to comprehend their motivations and emotions, preventing you from making judgments based on incomplete information. By genuinely caring and being interested, you foster a sense of trust and lessen the possibility of misunderstandings.

7. Reconsider Your Presumptions

To prevent drawing hasty conclusions, you must actively consider challenging your assumptions. Challenge any assumptions you may have about someone's intentions, feelings, or thoughts, and think of other possibilities instead. Think critically and assemble more information before making conclusions. This routine encourages accurate understanding and an open-minded approach to interactions.

8. Recognize confirmation bias.

The tendency to interpret information in a way that supports our preexisting beliefs or assumptions is known as confirmation bias. It can impair our judgment and cause misunderstandings. Be conscious of this bias and actively look for information to refute your preconceptions. Make an effort to gain a thorough understanding of the person and their behavior.

9. Develop cultural sensitivity

The capacity to communicate effectively and respectfully with people of other cultures is known as cultural competence. You can increase your awareness of cultural quirks, norms, and communication styles by becoming more culturally competent. You can approach cross-cultural interactions with sensitivity thanks to this awareness, preventing misunderstandings based on cultural stereotypes.

Conclusion

We have examined the nuances of human behavior, deciphered nonverbal cues, examined verbal communication, and developed emotional intelligence in this extensive guide on how to read people like a book. We have learned a lot along the way that will help us interpret the intricate web of human interaction with accuracy. Now that this investigation is over, it's critical to consider the main lessons learned and talk about how to keep improving our ability to read people.

Knowing the Value of People Reading: The capacity to read people is a valuable trait in many facets of life. Understanding the underlying emotions, intentions, and motives of others can significantly improve our interactions and decision-making, whether in personal relationships, professional settings, or social interactions. By improving our ability to read people, we gain a deeper comprehension of human nature and advance our communication and empathy abilities.

The Basics of People Reading: In the early chapters of this book, we examined the fundamentals of people reading by delving into body language, verbal cues, and emotional intelligence. We learned that reading a person's emotions and intentions through their posture, gestures, and facial expressions can be incredibly insightful. We also looked at the significance of speech patterns, vocal tonality, and emotional intelligence in correctly deciphering verbal communication.

Reading People in Various Contexts: As we progressed, we investigated the use of our people-reading abilities in various settings. By understanding nonverbal and verbal cues, we were better able to resolve conflicts, establish trust, and foster deeper connections in our personal relationships. We learned that reading people can be useful for assessing job candidates, comprehending coworkers, and improving leadership abilities in professional settings. Additionally, we investigated the subtleties of social interactions, developing our capacity to judge initial reactions, understand group dynamics, and adjust to various social contexts.

Advanced People-Reading Techniques: To improve our people-reading skills, we delved into advanced techniques like spotting deception and taking cultural and contextual considerations into account. We gained knowledge of how to read facial expressions, identify verbal and nonverbal cues to deception, and comprehend how cultural differences affect how we communicate. By diversifying our toolbox, we improved our ability to navigate challenging social situations while avoiding misunderstandings and presumptions.

Application in an ethical and responsible manner: Throughout this journey, we have emphasized the significance of using our people-reading abilities in an ethical and responsible manner. We must always respect others' right to privacy, avoid coercing others, and abstain from using our skills to hurt or deceive others. We work to uphold integrity, empathy, and fairness in our interactions while being conscious of the potential consequences of our interpretations and judgments.

Developing Your People Reading Skills: As we wrap up this book, it is important to recognize that developing your ability to read people is a lifelong process. Here are a few more pointers to help you improve your people-reading abilities:

1. Engage in active observation: Pay close attention to how those around you behave and analyze it. Pay close attention to verbal and nonverbal cues, listen intently when others are speaking, and take mental notes of any patterns or irregularities.

2. Seek Feedback and Validation: Have honest discussions with reliable people who can offer criticism on your interpretations and lend support to the validity of your understanding of people's behavior. Your skills will be improved and your perspective will be expanded thanks to this feedback loop.

3. Embrace Lifelong Learning: Continue to grow your knowledge by looking into new sources on communication, psychology, and body language. Attend seminars, courses, or workshops to improve your knowledge of human behavior.

4. Encourage Empathy: Develop your capacity to imagine yourself in another person's position. Demonstrate empathy by paying attention, expressing understanding, and expressing sincere interest in the thoughts and feelings of others. This will strengthen your relationships with people and improve your reading comprehension in general.

5. Apply and Reflect: Use your ability to read people in practical situations. Observe and evaluate how people behave in various situations, such as social gatherings, professional settings, or private interactions. Make a note of the results and consider whether your interpretations were correct. Gain knowledge from both accurate readings and any potential errors to hone your abilities and boost your accuracy over time.

Recognize the diversity of cultural norms and values in order to develop your cultural sensitivity. Be conscious of the impact that cultural backgrounds can have on nonverbal cues, communication methods, and behavior interpretations. Learn as much as you can about various cultures to prevent making assumptions or stereotyping people based on your limited knowledge.

7. Maintain an Open Mind: When interpreting others, keep an open mind. Stay away from making snap judgments or assumptions based on scant information. Recognize that people are complex, multifaceted beings, and that their behavior may be influenced by a variety of things like mood, circumstances in their personal lives, or previous experiences.

8. Develop Self-Awareness: Recognize that your perceptions of other people can be influenced by your own prejudices, beliefs, and emotions. Develop self-awareness and mindfulness to become aware of and manage any biases you may have that could skew your readings. Try to maintain an impartial viewpoint and objectivity.

9. Constantly Improve Your Communication Skills: Understanding people well requires effective communication. By engaging in active listening exercises, working on your verbal and nonverbal expressions, and being conscious of how your actions may be perceived by others, you can improve your own communication skills.

10. Seek Feedback and Learn from Mistakes: Be open to other people's feedback and take lessons from any errors or misunderstandings you may have. You can improve as a people reader and gain insightful information from constructive criticism. Adopt a growth mindset and see every experience as a chance to get better.

Keep in mind that mastering the art of reading people is a process rather than a finish line. It necessitates constant commitment, exercise, and introspection. You can become a skilled people reader, unlocking a richer understanding of the human experience and fostering deeper connections in all spheres of your life, by continually honing your abilities, seeking to understand others with empathy, and upholding ethical principles.

As we come to the end of this book, I want to encourage you to use the power of reading people ethically and responsibly to improve your relationships, your communication abilities, and your understanding of the human mind. May your development as a skilled people reader be fruitful in understanding, expansion, and beneficial impact.

www.ingramcontent.com/pod-product-compliance
Lightning Source LLC
Chambersburg PA
CBHW050339290526
45785CB00006B/2563